R
It
w

E
B
C
E
G

feeling WORRIED!

First published in 2017 by Wayland

Text copyright © Wayland 2017
Illustrations copyright © Mike Gordon 2017

Wayland
Carmelite House
50 Victoria Embankment
London EC4Y 0DZ

Wayland Australia
Level 17/207 Kent Street
Sydney, NSW 2000

Managing editor: Victoria Brooker
Creative design: Paul Cherrill

ISBN: 978 1 5263 0073 7

Printed in China

Wayland is a division of
Hachette Children's Books,
an Hachette UK company.
www.hachette.co.uk

Feeling WORRIED!

Written by
Kay Barnham

Illustrated by
Mike Gordon

WAYLAND

School was finished for the day and the long, summer afternoon lay ahead. "As soon as I get home, I'm going to play on my scooter," Annie said.

"Lucky you," said her little brother Jamie. "I've got to do my maths homework."

4

"Oh, that won't take you long," said Annie.
She couldn't believe it when a tear rolled
down Jamie's cheek.

"What's wrong?" said Annie. She hated it
when her brother was upset.
"The homework looks really, really difficult,"
sobbed Jamie. "I keep looking at it and I don't
know what I'm supposed to do. I'm so worried.
Mrs Skinner will be so cross with me."

"Don't worry, Jamie," said Annie. "We'll look at the homework together. It might not be as tricky as you think."

Ten minutes later, they sat in the kitchen. "Let's check out the first question," said Annie. "Look, all you have to do is add those numbers and then multiply them by 5." "That's all?" asked Jamie.

"That's all," said Annie.

"And I've spent all week worrying about it ..."
said Jamie, rolling his eyes.
"Next time, I'll just have a go!"

At school the next day, Annie heard some
very sad news. Riley's parents were splitting up.
"Are you OK?" she asked Riley.

"Not really," said Riley. "I love my mum and dad. Now, I don't know which one I'm going to live with. And I'm just so worried that I won't get to see them both."

Annie frowned. She didn't know what would happen either. "Have you asked your mum and dad about it?" she said.

Riley shook her head.
"Go on," said Annie. "They both love you.
They might even be able to make you feel
better with some answers."

The next day,
Riley looked a little happier.
 "Did you ask your parents
about the separation?" said Annie.

Riley nodded. "They told me that
I'll live with mum, but I'll stay with my dad every
Wednesday and every other weekend.
I'll see him in the holidays too. I'm so pleased
I spoke to them."

The week after half term, Mrs Skinner had a surprise for the class— a brand new pupil!
  "Let me introduce you to Amelia," said the teacher. "She's moved here from the USA. Please make her feel welcome."

Annie smiled at the new girl,
but Amelia barely looked up.

Even though everyone tried to talk to Amelia, the new girl just shrugged and wouldn't speak. Soon, most of them stopped trying. But Annie was determined to help.

"What's wrong?"
Annie asked Amelia.
"Nothing," mumbled the
new girl. She twisted a
plait round her finger.
"Really?" said Annie.
"OK, I'm worried
everyone will laugh
at me when I speak,"
she said at last.

19

"What's wrong with the way you speak?"
said Annie, puzzled.
"Well, nothing," said Amelia. "But I come
from another country. So that means I speak
differently to everyone else in this school.
They'll think I sound odd."

"So that's why you've been quiet!" Annie said.
"Well, I think you sound *great*," she said.

"Now come and meet my friends. And don't worry.
They'll love your accent too, I promise."

That evening, it was Annie's turn to feel worried.
Tomorrow, she and Jamie were going to visit
the dentist with Dad. And she was not
looking forward to it *at all*.

What if the dentist wanted to poke about in her teeth? What if he told her off for not brushing enough? What if he told her she needed a filling?

The next morning, Annie
was still worried.

"What's wrong?" asked
Mum at breakfast time.
Why aren't you eating?
Are you feeling poorly?"

24

Annie stared at her meal. "I'm worried about going to the dentist," she admitted. "And my stomach is churning so much that I don't feel even a little bit hungry."

"Come on, eat up. The dentist is there
to look after your teeth, not to shout at you,"
said Mum. "You can brush your teeth before we
go. But first, I have an idea..."

After breakfast, Mum pretended to be
the dentist, while Annie was the patient.
It was great fun. Soon, they were laughing
so much that Jamie demanded to join in too.
And then so did Dad.

Later that morning, the real dentist didn't seem half so scary. When she sat in the dentist's chair, Annie pictured her mum pretending to be a dentist and that made her forget her worry.

"What a terrific patient you are," the dentist said.
"I was a bit worried," Annie admitted, "but then
I remembered something really funny and that
made me feel better."

"Excellent," said the dentist. "It's so much
easier to check someone's teeth
when they are smiling."

FURTHER INFORMATION

THINGS TO DO

1. A frown can show that someone is worried.
A smile can show that someone is happy.

Scientists can't agree whether frowning or smiling uses
more muscles. Try frowning and then smiling and see what
you think the answer is.

2. Draw a picture of yourself, adding as many pencil frown
lines as you can. Now rub out the frown lines and watch your
worries magically disappear!

3. Make a colourful word cloud! Start with 'worried', then add
any other words this makes you think of. Write them all down
using different coloured pens. More important words
should be bigger, less important words smaller.
Start like this...

NERVOUS worried

nail-biting

NOTES FOR PARENTS AND TEACHERS

The aim of this book is to help children think about their feelings in an enjoyable, interactive way. Encourage them to have fun pointing to the illustrations, making sounds and acting, too. Here are more specific ideas for getting more out of the book:

Encourage children to talk about their own feelings, if they feel comfortable doing so, either while you are reading the book or afterwards. Here are some conversation prompts to try:

What makes you feel worried?
How do you stop feeling worried when this happens?

2. Make a facemask that shows a worried expression.

3. Put on a feelings play! Ask groups of children to act out the different scenarios in the book. The children could use their facemasks to show when they are worried in the play.

4. Hold a worried-face competition. Who can look the MOST worried?! Strictly no laughing allowed!

BOOKS TO SHARE

A Book of Feelings
by Amanda McCardie, illustrated by Salvatore Rubbino
(Walker, 2016)

But What If?
by Sue Graves, illustrated by Desideria Guicciardini
(Franklin Watts, 2015)

I'm Worried by Brian Moses, illustrated by Mike Gordon
(Wayland, 1998)

Mum and Dad Glue by Kes Gray, illustrated by Lee Wildish
(Hodder, 2015)

The Huge Bag of Worries
by Virginia Ironside, illustrated by Frank Rodgers
(Hodder Children's Books, 2011)

Dinosaurs Have Feelings, Too: William Worrysaurus
by Brian Moses, illustrated by Mike Gordon
(Wayland, 2015)

READ ALL THE BOOKS
IN THIS SERIES:

Feeling Angry!
ISBN: 978 1 5263 0015 7

Feeling Frightened!
ISBN: 978 1 5263 0077 5

Feeling Jealous!
ISBN: 978 1 5263 0075 1

Feeling Sad!
ISBN: 978 1 5263 0071 3

Feeling Shy!
ISBN: 978 1 5263 0079 9

Feeling Worried!
ISBN: 978 1 5263 0073 7